ISBN 0.7119.1516.4 Order No. OP 44825

Exclusive distributors:
BOOK SALES LIMITED
8/9 Frith Street, London W1V 5TZ, UK.
MUSIC SALES CORPORATION
24 East 22nd Street, New York, NY 10010, USA.
MUSIC SALES PTY LIMITED
120 Rothschild Street, Roseberry, NSW 2018, Australia.
To the Music Trade only:
MUSIC SALES LIMITED
8/9 Frith Street, London W1V 5TZ, UK.

Editorial Research by Susan Black.
Far East Tour Report by James Manning.
Book Designed by Mainartery.
Picture Research by Mary McCartney and James Manning..
Picture credits: London Features International, Pictorial Press Ltd., Ross Barnett, Serge Thomann.
Typeset by Capital Setters, London.
Printed in England by Scotprint, Musselburgh, Scotland.

Omnibus Press
London/New York/Sydney/Cologne

MICHAEL JACKSON

'Ever since Michael was very young, he seemed different to me from the rest of the children,' says Katherine Jackson, Michael's mother. 'I don't believe in reincarnation, but you know how babies move uncoordinated? He never moved that way. When he danced, it was like he was an older person.'

'Little Michael knew who he was from the very beginning,' agrees Gladys Johnson, his kindergarten teacher. 'When he was five years old and had a little difficulty with his arithmetic, he told the teacher, "Oh, I don't need to learn those numbers. My manager will count my money." It was sort of frightening. He was so young. He didn't go out and play much. So if you want me to tell the truth, I don't know where he got it. He just *knew*.'

Two and a half decades later Michael Jackson stands in triumph as the most successful performer in the history of popular music. Other artists may have spread a greater influence - Presley in the fifties, The Beatles in the sixties, even The Sex Pistols in the seventies - but no singer can match the sheer *numbers* that Jackson has accumulated.

Michael has now sold out eight concerts at London's 80,000 seater Wembley stadium, thus setting a new record for an unbroken run at the UK's biggest venue that is unlikely ever to be broken again. Previously the record – four nights – was held by Genesis with Bruce Springsteen and Madonna (three each), and David Bowie and U2 (two each) trailing behind.

But this record is dwarfed by the ongoing success of Michael's 1982 album 'Thriller' which, with sales now topping the 35 million mark, is far and away the most successful LP in the history of the music business. Whichever album comes second – and there are many contenders – it is at least ten million copies behind Michael's landmark figure.

By Michael's standards, then, it could be implied that 'Bad', released in September of 1987, is a relative failure in that it hasn't – and probably won't – attain such sales figures. Nevertheless, it will unquestionably be amongst the best selling LPs of the eighties, just as 'Off The Wall', Michael's first solo album since leaving Tamla-Motown, became one of the best selling LPs of the seventies, shifting some eight million copies and becoming CBS's best selling LP ever (up to that time) in the process.

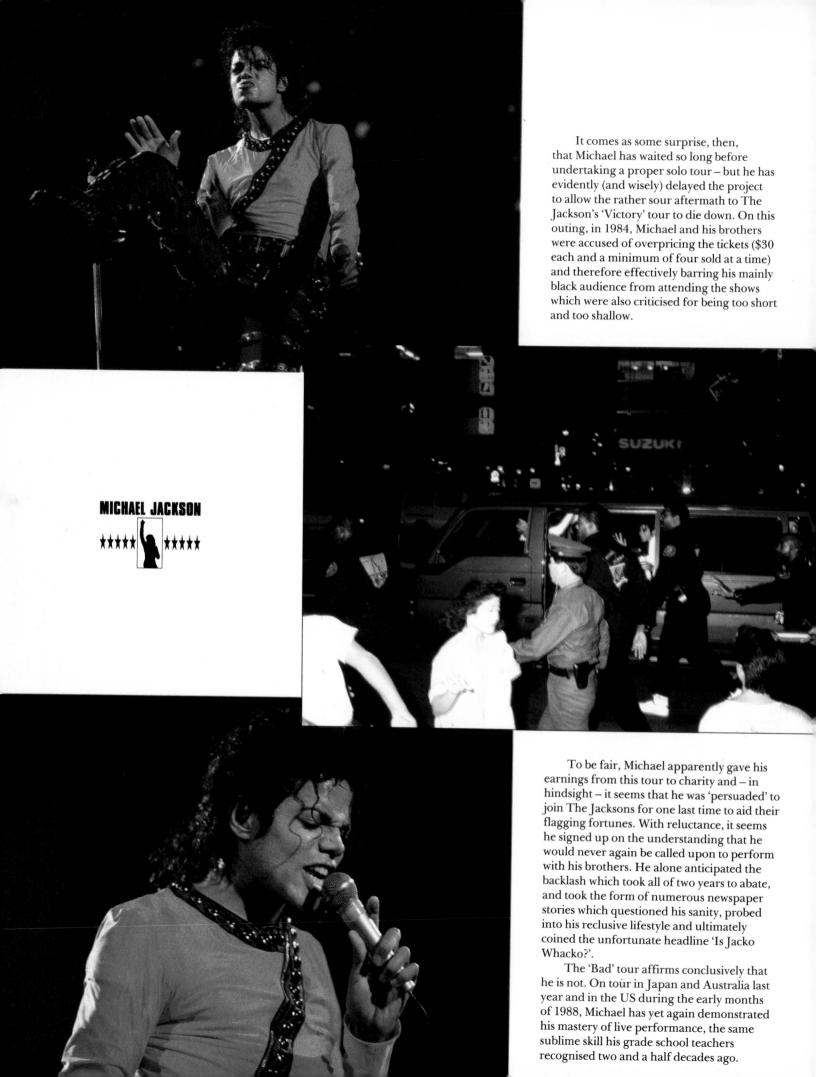

MICHAEL JACKSON

★★★★★ ★★★★★

It comes as some surprise, then, that Michael has waited so long before undertaking a proper solo tour – but he has evidently (and wisely) delayed the project to allow the rather sour aftermath to The Jackson's 'Victory' tour to die down. On this outing, in 1984, Michael and his brothers were accused of overpricing the tickets ($30 each and a minimum of four sold at a time) and therefore effectively barring his mainly black audience from attending the shows which were also criticised for being too short and too shallow.

To be fair, Michael apparently gave his earnings from this tour to charity and – in hindsight – it seems that he was 'persuaded' to join The Jacksons for one last time to aid their flagging fortunes. With reluctance, it seems he signed up on the understanding that he would never again be called upon to perform with his brothers. He alone anticipated the backlash which took all of two years to abate, and took the form of numerous newspaper stories which questioned his sanity, probed into his reclusive lifestyle and ultimately coined the unfortunate headline 'Is Jacko Whacko?'.

The 'Bad' tour affirms conclusively that he is not. On tour in Japan and Australia last year and in the US during the early months of 1988, Michael has yet again demonstrated his mastery of live performance, the same sublime skill his grade school teachers recognised two and a half decades ago.

MICHAEL JACKSON

FACTS:

Birthdate: August 29, 1958.

Birthplace: Gary, Indiana, USA.

Parents' names: Joseph and Katherine Jackson.

Brothers and sisters: Maureen (born 1950), Sigmund Esco 'Jackie' (1951), Toriano Adaryl 'Tito' (1953), Jermaine (1954), LaToya (1955), Marlon (1957), Randy (1961), Janet (1967).

First public appearance: Singing 'Climb Every Mountain' in class at Garnett Elementary School as a five-year-old.

First record bought: 'Mickey's Monkey' by The Miracles, written by Holland-Dozier-Holland.

First break: Winning Gary's first ever City Wide Talent Show in 1965.

First group: Ripples and Waves Plus Michael (which became The Jackson 5).

First record 'Big Boy'/'You've Changed' on Steeltown Records, a local Gary label.

Acts for whom the Jackson 5 opened before singing with Tamla-Motown: The Temptations, Etta James, James Brown, Gladys Knight & The Pips, The Chi-Lites, The Emotions, The O'Jays, Jackie Wilson, Jerry Butler, Sam & Dave and others.

First manager: Joe Jackson (Michael's father). Joe attempted to sell a 50% share in the Jackson 5's management to Sam Moore (of Sam & Dave) for $500.00 in 1968 but Sam turned him down. Joe later went into business with Richard Arons, a New York lawyer.

Second record label: Tamla-Motown in Detroit. The Jackson 5 was introduced to Motown by Gladys Knight (although Diana Ross later took the credit).

First Tamla-Motown hit: 'I Want You Back'/ 'Who's Loving You' written by 'The Corporation' (Berry Gordy, Freddie Perren, Lawrence Mizell and Deke Richards) in October 1969.

First TV appearance: ABC's Hollywood Special, hosted by Diana Ross, October 18, 1969.

MICHAEL JACKSON
★★★★★ ★★★★★

First TV special: Goin' Back To Indiana,
based around The Jackson 5's homecoming
to Gary on January 31, 1971, starring Tom
Smothers, Bill Cosby, Bobby Darin and
Diana Ross.

First world tour: 1972, visiting Europe,
Japan and West Africa. (Michael's first ever
appearance in London was with his brothers
at the Talk Of The Town nightclub – now
The Hippodrome – before an audience of
press and radio people.)

First home outside Gary: When The Jackson 5
moved to California in 1969 the family was
split up – half living with Motown chief Berry
Gordy and half, including Michael, at Diana
Ross's house. Later the whole family moved
into a mansion at Encino which Michael
still owns.

First album: 'Diana Ross Presents The
Jackson 5', Tamla-Motown, April 1970.

First solo single: 'Got To Be There',
Tamla-Motown, January 1972.

First solo LP: 'Got To Be There',
Tamla-Motown.

First feature film: Save The Children, a
documentary about Jesse Jackson's Operation
PUSH in Chicago which also featured Gladys
Knight, The Temptations, Sammy Davis Jnr.,
Marvin Gaye, and Isaac Hayes.

Solo film debut: The Wiz, in 1978, also
starring Diana Ross.

First solo number one hit: 'Ben'
(USA, November 1972).

Current record label: Epic.

Best selling solo LP: 'Thriller' (December,
1982), which has gone on to sell over 35
million copies throughout the world making
it the best selling LP in the history of the
record industry.

Favourite book: Peter Pan, by J.M. Barrie.

Favourite film: E.T.

Instruments played: Keyboards and drums.

Duets: Michael has recorded duets with Diana
Ross, Marvin Gaye and Paul McCartney.

Height: 5ft 9ins.

Weight: 110 lbs.

Eyes: dark brown.

FAR EAST TOUR REPORT

For any major artist or group about to begin a world tour, Japan provides an excellent stage for the final live dress rehearsal.

An artist can iron out any problems in the stage show without the worry of criticism from the press. The media coverage of pop acts in Japan seems only to idolise its subjects. The country seems to have an insatiable thirst for western pop acts.

Recently George Michael started his long-awaited world solo tour in Japan. So too did Madonna – and so intense was the demand for her tickets the promoters had to return about three million pounds to unsuccessful applicants for mail-order seats!

Even Mick Jagger, currently struggling under a "mid-life career crisis" according to Robert Hilburn in the LA Times, can make a fist of it in Tokyo. It was almost as if the Japanese audiences didn't realise the rest of the Rolling Stones don't turn up with Mick Jagger, solo artist.

So it should have been no surprise that one of the most astute pop artists ever, Michael Jackson, should decide to launch his live solo career in Japan.

Jackson, knowing that many expected him to fall flat on his face with the 'Bad' album, and subsequent tour, wanted to prove them wrong.

MICHAEL JACKSON

MICHAEL JACKSON'S BAND

Bass	—	Don Boyette
Drums	—	Ricky Lawson
Guitars	—	Jennifer Batten
		Jon Clark
Keyboards	—	Chris Currell
		Rory Kaplan
		Greg Phillinganes
Singers	—	Sheryl Crow
		Kevin Dorsey
		Dorian Holley
		Darryl Phinnessee
Dancers	—	Randy Allaire
		Evaldo Garcia
		Dominic Lucero
		La Velle Smith

✯✯✯✯✯

✯✯✯✯✯

Michael Jackson finally made it to Japan in September of 1987 – and there was certainly no lack of media interest. When his Japan Airlines Flight 61 touched down at Tokyo's Narita Airport there were no less than 600 journalists and cameramen waiting to cover the event. Some 300 even turned up when his pet chimp Bubbles arrived on a separate flight!

Similarly some 300 turned out for his press conference and the ubiquitous Australian pop "guru", Molly Meldrum, flew in and recorded a world exclusive interview (shown on the TV program 60 Minutes). Meldrum, however, failed to elicit much more than a nod or a monosyllable from Michael in response to each question, rendering the interview brief and non-informative. In fact while Michael remained mostly silent his manager, the cigar-chomping Frank Dileo, answered or skilfully avoided virtually all of Molly's probing questions.

When the actual concerts began, however, perhaps the biggest surprise of all was the sheer brilliance of Jackson's performance. The man who hadn't performed live since the Jackson's Victory Tour back in 1984 stunned audiences across Japan, Australia and the United States, quickly dispelling any doubts concerning his diminishing popularity.

The show – which didn't alter very much from night to night – was a tightly packed two hours of Michael's best material.

One of the tour's biggest criticisms was that he didn't play enough material from his younger days. He did, however, showcase a medley of three songs – "I Want You Back", "The Love You Save" and "I'll Be There" – but that only left the audience crying for more.

The bulk of the remainder of the material was taken from the albums 'Off The Wall', 'Thriller' and 'Bad'.

The songs included "Wanna Be Startin' Something" – a song that opens each concert and a number that Whitney Houston used for a long time to begin her shows. Others from 'Thriller' included "Beat It" (which begins just as Michael pulls his amazing disappearing act that virtually defies description), "Billie Jean" and, of course, "Thriller" itself which involved Michael and four dancers in a rigorous workout.

From 'Bad' came the title track – usually the concert's final song, "I Just Can't Stop Loving You" (which features a duet with backing singer Sheryl Crow) and "The Way You Make Me Feel".

Audiences in Japan and Australia missed out on a live version of the brilliant "Man In The Mirror" – they had to settle for the live performance he gave on the 1988 Grammy Show. But for his American concerts Michael has added this song.

And make no mistake – Michael Jackson live is a sexy, sensual performer. He bumps and grinds most limbs of his body in a way that makes George Michael and Prince look tame.

Michael dances with as much power and restrained energy as when he sings. Once you see him swirling about the stage you begin to believe the stories about the marathon practice sessions in dance studios. He constantly twists and turns effortlessly and even when he hinted at "moonwalking" everybody went bonkers. When he actually does it's magic.

His stage costumes range from the belt buckled black outfit he wore on the cover of 'Bad' to a glittery silver jump suit. He also appears in an assortment of hats, capes, boots, studded wristbands and, of course, the infamous glove!

MICHAEL JACKSON

The eleven-member band and four dancers all wear a variety of outfits. Most of the time they seem to resemble the goonish streetlife that lurks in the corners of Michael Jackson videos.

His stage performance, the songs and how they were packaged, added up to an extremely successful fourteen-date tour of Japan and a five-date tour of Australia. Due to various problems, shows in some Australian states and New Zealand had to be cancelled.

At one of Michael's Brisbane shows he was joined onstage by Stevie Wonder who was touring Australia at the same time. For years Stevie appeared alongside Michael as a member of the Motown family (Stevie is still with the label). More recently he sang a duet with Michael, "Just Good Friends", which was written by Australian songwriters Terry Britten and Graham Lyle for the 'Bad' album.

When not onstage in Australia, Michael spent time visiting sick children in hospitals and on one memorable occasion even visited two children at their home in surburban Sydney. He actually put them to bed after a plea over the phone from the childrens' mother!

One of Michael's other passions in life is shopping. While the stores of Japan and Australia were tempting, his biggest spending spree during the initial days of the World Tour was saved for a special trip he made to Hong Kong.

While Michael Jackson at times appears to be the world's most elusive artist, he is, at the same time, the most accessible through the universal appeal of his music.

Even though Michael is not one of music's most prolific acts – one can be sure that the rest of his career will probably be as weird and as wonderful as it currently is.

James Manning, Smash Hits, Sydney

MICHAEL JACKSON

Discography

7" SINGLES

GOT TO BE THERE/MARIA (YOU WERE THE ONLY
ONE)
Tamla Motown TMG 797
January 1972

ROCKIN' ROBIN/LOVE IS HERE & NOW YOU'RE GONE
Tamla Motown TMG 816
May 1972

AIN'T NO SUNSHINE/I WANNA BE WHERE YOU ARE
Tamla Motown TMG 826
July 1972

BEN/YOU CAN CRY ON MY SHOULDER
Tamla Motown TMG 834
November 1972

MORNING GLOW/MY GIRL
Tamla Motown TMG 863
July 1973

MUSIC AND ME/JOHNNY RAVEN
Tamla Motown TMG 900
May 1974

ONE DAY IN YOUR LIFE/WITH A CHILD'S HEART
Tamla Motown TMG 946
April 1975

JUST A LITTLE BIT OF YOU/DEAR MICHAEL
Tamla Motown TMG 1006
October 1975

EASE ON DOWN THE ROAD (WITH DIANA ROSS)/
POPPY GIRLS
B-side by Diana Ross
MCA MCA 396
October 1978

YOU CAN'T WIN (PART 1)/YOU CAN'T WIN (PART 2)
Epic EPC 7135
May 1979

YOU CAN'T WIN (PART 1)/YOU CAN'T WIN (PART 2)
Picture disc
Epic EPC 7135
May 1979

DON'T STOP 'TIL YOU GET ENOUGH/I CAN'T HELP IT
Epic EPC 7763
August 1979

OFF THE WALL/WORKING DAY AND NIGHT
Epic EPC 8045
November 1979

ROCK WITH YOU/GET ON THE FLOOR
Epic EPC 8206
February 1980

SHE'S OUT OF MY LIFE/PUSH ME AWAY
B-side by Jacksons
Epic EPC 8384
April 1980

BEN/ABRAHAM MARTIN & JOHN
B-side by Marvin Gaye
Motown TMG 1165
April 1980

GIRLFRIEND/BLESS HIS SOUL
B-side by Jacksons
Epic EPC 8782
July 1980

GOT TO BE THERE/I MISS YOU BABY
B-side by Marv Johnson
Motown TMG 973
October 1980

WE'RE ALMOST THERE/WE'VE GOT A GOOD THING
GOING
Motown TMG 977
July 1981

ROCKIN' ROBIN/LOVE IS HERE & NOW YOU'RE GONE
(REISSUE)
Motown TMG 816
October 1981

AIN'T NO SUNSHINE/I WANNA BE WHERE YOU ARE
(REISSUE)
Motown TMG 826
October 1981

BEN/YOU CAN CRY ON MY SHOULDER (REISSUE)
Motown TMG 834
October 1981

GOT TO BE THERE/I MISS YOU BABY (REISSUE)
B-side by Marv Johnson
Motown TMG 973
October 1981

ONE DAY IN YOUR LIFE/TAKE ME BACK (REISSUE)
Motown TMG 976
October 1981

WE'RE ALMOST THERE/WE'VE GOT A GOOD THING
GOING (REISSUE)
Motown TMG 977
October 1981

BEN/ABRAHAM MARTIN & JOHN (REISSUE)
B-side by Marvin Gaye
Motown TMG 1165
October 1981

OFF THE WALL/WORKING DAY AND NIGHT (REISSUE)
Epic EPC 8045
April 1982

ROCK WITH YOU/GET ON THE FLOOR (REISSUE)
Epic EPC 8206
April 1982

OFF THE WALL/DON'T STOP 'TIL YOU GET ENOUGH
Epic EPC 8856
April 1982

THE GIRL IS MINE (WITH PAUL MCCARTNEY)/
CAN'T GET OUTTA THE RAIN
Epic EPC A 2729
October 1982

THE GIRL IS MINE (WITH PAUL MCCARTNEY)/
CAN'T GET OUTTA THE RAIN
Picture disc
Epic EPC A 2729
October 1982

BILLIE JEAN/IT'S THE FALLING IN LOVE
Epic EPC A 3084
January 1983

BEAT IT/BURN THIS DISCO OUT
Epic EPC A 3258
March 1983

ONE DAY IN YOUR LIFE/TAKE ME BACK (REISSUE)
Motown TMG 976
April 1983

WE'RE ALMOST THERE/WE'VE GOT A GOOD THING
GOING (REISSUE)
Motown TMG 977
April 1983

WANNA BE STARTIN' SOMETHING/ROCK WITH YOU
Epic EPC A 3427
June 1983

HAPPY/WE'RE ALMOST THERE
Motown TMG 986
July 1983

HAPPY/WE'RE ALMOST THERE
Picture disc
Motown TMGP 986
July 1983

SAY SAY SAY (WITH PAUL MCCARTNEY)/
ODE TO A KOALA BEAR
B-side by Paul McCartney
Parlophone R 6062
October 1983

THRILLER/THINGS I DO FOR YOU
Epic EPC A 3643
November 1983

MICHAEL JACKSON 9 SINGLES PACK
(includes red vinyl copies of "Don't Stop 'Til You
Get Enough", "Off The Wall", "Rock With You",
"She's Out Of My Life", "The Girl Is Mine", "Billie
Jean", "Beat It", "Wanna Be Startin' Something"
and "Thriller")
Epic MJ1
November 1983

P.Y.T. (PRETTY YOUNG THING)/HEARTBREAK HOTEL
Epic EPC A 4136
March 1984

FAREWELL MY SUMMER LOVE/CALL ON ME
Motown TMG 1342
May 1984

EASE ON DOWN THE ROAD (WITH DIANA ROSS)/
POPPY GIRLS (REISSUE)
B-side by Diana Ross
MCA MCA 896
July 1984

GIRL YOU'RE SO TOGETHER/TOUCH THE ONE YOU
LOVE
Motown TMG 1355
August 1984

GOT TO BE THERE/ROCKIN' ROBIN (REISSUE)
Motown TMG 994
April 1985

I JUST CAN'T STOP LOVING YOU (WITH SIEDAH
GARRETT)/BABY BE MINE
Epic 650 202 7
July 1987

I JUST CAN'T STOP LOVING YOU (WITH SIEDAH
GARRETT)/BABY BE MINE
Issued in poster bag
Epic 650 202 0
July 1987

BAD/BAD (DANCE REMIX RADIO EDIT)
Epic 651 155 7
September 1987

I SAW MOMMY KISSING SANTA CLAUS/SANTA CLAUS
IS COMING TO TOWN
Motown ZB 41655
November 1987

THE WAY YOU MAKE ME FEEL/THE WAY YOU MAKE
ME FEEL (DUB MIX)
Epic 651 275 7
November 1987

MAN IN THE MIRROR/MAN IN THE MIRROR
(INSTRUMENTAL)
Epic 651 388 7
February 1988

MAN IN THE MIRROR/MAN IN THE MIRROR
(INSTRUMENTAL)
Shaped picture disc
Epic 651 388 9
February 1988

I WANT YOU BACK/NEVER CAN SAY GOODBYE
Tamla Motown ZB 41913
April 1988

12" SINGLES

EASE ON DOWN THE ROAD (WITH DIANA ROSS)/
POPPY GIRLS
B-side is by Diana Ross
MCA 12-396
October 1978

YOU CAN'T WIN (PART 1)/YOU CAN'T WIN (PART 2)
Epic 12EPC 7135
May 1979

ROCK WITH YOU/GET ON THE FLOOR
Epic 12EPC 8206
February 1980

WE'RE ALMOST THERE/WE'VE GOT A GOOD THING
GOING
Motown TMGT 977
July 1981

WE'RE ALMOST THERE/WE'VE GOT A GOOD THING
GOING (REISSUE)
Motown TMGT 977
October 1981

BILLIE JEAN/IT'S THE FALLING IN LOVE
Epic EPC A13 3084
January 1983

BEAT IT/BURN THIS DISCO OUT
Epic EPC TA 3258
March 1983

WANNA BE STARTIN' SOMETHING/ROCK WITH YOU/
WANNA BE STARTIN' SOMETHING (INSTRUMENTAL)
Epic TA 3427
June 1983

HAPPY/WE'RE ALMOST THERE
Motown TMGT 986
July 1983

SAY SAY SAY (WITH PAUL McCARTNEY)/SAY SAY SAY
(INSTRUMENTAL)/ODE TO A KOALA BEAR
'Ode To A Koala Bear' is by Paul McCartney
Parlophone 12R 6062
October 1983

THRILLER (REMIX)/THINGS I DO FOR YOU/THRILLER
With free calendar
Epic TA 3643
November 1983

P.Y.T. (PRETTY YOUNG THING/THIS PLACE HOTEL/
THRILLER (INSTRUMENTAL)
Epic TA 4136
March 1984

EASE ON DOWN THE ROAD(WITH DIANA ROSS)/POPPY
GIRLS
B-side is by Diana Ross
Reissue
MCA MCAT 898
May 1984

FAREWELL MY SUMMER LOVE/CALL ON ME
Motown TMGT 1342
May 1984

GIRL YOU'RE SO TOGETHER/TOUCH THE ONE YOU
LOVE/BEN/AIN'T NO SUNSHINE
Motown TMGT 1355
August 1984

WE'RE ALMOST THERE/WE'VE GOT A GOOD THING
GOING (REISSUE)
Motown TMGT 977
April 1985

GOT TO BE THERE/ROCKIN' ROBIN
Motown TMGT 994
April 1985

I JUST CAN'T STOP LOVING YOU (WITH SIEDAH
GARRETT)/BABY BE MINE/LOVE GAMES
Epic 650 202 6
July 1987

BAD (EXTENDED)/BAD (REMIX)/BAD (INSTRUMENTAL
REMIX)
Epic 651 155 0
September 1987

BAD (DANCE EXTENDED MIX WITH FALSE FADE)/BAD
(DUB MIX)/BAD (A CAPPELLA)
Epic 651 155 6
September 1987

THE WAY YOU MAKE ME FEEL (EXTENDED)/THE WAY
YOU MAKE ME FEEL/THE WAY YOU MAKE ME FEEL
(DUB MIX)
Epic 651 275 6
November 1987

MAN IN THE MIRROR/MAN IN THE MIRROR (REMIX)/
MAN IN THE MIRROR (INSTRUMENTAL)
Epic 651 388 6
February 1988

I WANT YOU BACK (12" REMIX)/(ORIGINAL MIX)/(YOU
KNOW WE GOT SOUL DUB MIX)/NEVER CAN SAY
GOODBYE
Tamla Motown ZT 41914
April 1988

7" EPs

GREATEST ORIGINAL HITS
Epic EPC 2906
March 1983

CASSETTE SINGLES

MICHAEL JACKSON
Epic EPC A40 2627
August 1982

GREATEST ORIGINAL HITS
Epic EPC A40 2906
December 1982

MOTOWN FLIP HITS – MICHAEL JACKSON
Motown CTME 2035
July 1983

THE 12" TAPE
Epic EPC 4501274
September 1986

BAD
Epic 651 155 4
September 1987

CD SINGLES

THE WAY YOU MAKE ME FEEL
Epic 651 275 9
November 1987

MAN IN THE MIRROR
Epic 651 388 2
February 1988

LPs

GOT TO BE THERE
Tamla Motown STML 11205
May 1972

BEN
Tamla Motown STML 11220
December 1972

MUSIC AND ME
Tamla Motown STML 11235
July 1973

FOREVER, MICHAEL
Tamla Motown STMA 8022
March 1975

THE BEST OF MICHAEL JACKSON
Tamla Motown STML 12005
September 1975

OFF THE WALL
Epic EPC 83468
August 1979

ONE DAY IN YOUR LIFE
Motown STML 12158
July 1981

GOT TO BE THERE (REISSUE)
Motown STMS 5007
October 1981

ONE DAY IN YOUR LIFE (REISSUE)
Motown STML 12158
October 1981

AIN'T NO SUNSHINE
Pickwick TMS 3511
October 1982

THRILLER
Epic EPC 85930
December 1982

THRILLER
Picture disc
Epic EPC 11-85930
December 1982

FOREVER, MICHAEL (REISSUE)
Motown STMS 5095
June 1983

18 GREATEST HITS OF MICHAEL JACKSON & THE
JACKSON 5
Telstar STAR 2232
July 1983

MICHAEL JACKSON & THE JACKSON 5 GREATEST HITS
Motown WL 72087
April 1984

BEN (REISSUE)
Motown WL 72069
May 1984

FAREWELL MY SUMMER LOVE
Motown ZL 72227
August 1984

GREAT LOVE SONGS OF MICHAEL JACKSON
Motown WL 72289
November 1984

MUSIC AND ME (REISSUE)
Motown WL 72291
November 1984

LOOKING BACK TO YESTERDAY (NEVER BEFORE
RELEASED MASTERS)
Motown WL 72424
May 1986

OFF THE WALL (REISSUE)
Epic 450086 1
November 1986

BAD
Epic 450290 1
September 1987

LOVE SONGS
Telstar STAR 2298
October 1987

THE MICHAEL JACKSON MIX
Stylus SMR 745
December 1987

CDs

OFF THE WALL
Epic CDEPC 83468
1983

THRILLER
Epic CDEPC 85930
December 1983

18 GREATEST HITS OF MICHAEL JACKSON &
THE JACKSON 5
Motown MCD 06070 MD
May 1984

THE VERY BEST OF MICHAEL JACKSON & THE
JACKSON 5
Telstar TCD 2232
July 1986

GOT TO BE THERE/BEN
Motown ZD 72468
November 1986

ANTHOLOGY
Motown ZD 72530
January 1987

BAD
Epic 450290 2
September 1987

THE MICHAEL JACKSON MIX
Stylus SMD 745
December 1987

JLS

ANNUAL 2012

Posy Edwards

Since they first met, life has been an emotional rollercoaster for Aston, Marvin, JB and Oritsé. The four talented youngsters poured hundreds of hours into rehearsals, but caught their big break when they appeared on *X Factor*, catapulting them into the public eye. They might have come second in the contest, but you couldn't say they had lost out.

After being signed to Epic Records, the boys have released a string of number one hit singles, released two smash hit albums, played to thousands of screaming fans across the UK, and started in their quest to conquer America. Phew! How on earth do they find the time?

JLS have always had a strong work ethic. 'When we first got together we wrote a list of over 300 things we wanted to achieve and every time we met up to rehearse we would go through it and focus on what we would accomplish that week,' says Oritsé. 'We weren't messing around – it was all or nothing!'

PRINCES OF POP!

And the boys have stuck to that determination to make the best pop music they can and to reward their fans for supporting them throughout their short career. These four boys have got their feet firmly on the ground, though they're one of the biggest boybands on the planet right now! And one of the things that keeps them together is their friendship. 'I think people can see the genuine bond we have between us,' says Marvin. 'We genuinely are best friends and genuinely love what we do and that's something you can't manufacture. It's real.'

No pretenders to the throne, JLS are the crown princes of pop. Let the good times roll! Read on to find out all the JLS pop secrets and gossip, plus some awesome activities and gorgeous pictures of the hottest guys on the block … Swoon!

Chapter 1
Who are these guys?

HELLO ASTON!

Aston Merrygold was born on 13th February 1988. He's one of seven children, with one sister and five brothers – that's one big family! Aston, who was nicknamed Li'l Man at school, is the hyperactive member of JLS – and proof that good things come in small packages! His favourite breakfast is a combo of porridge and fruit and the first record he ever bought was *My Way* by Usher. Aston had always known he wanted to get into performing from a young age – he left school at age 16 and appeared on stage and in several TV shows. While attending an audition Aston made friends with Marvin, which eventually led to his JLS call!

Favourite thing about being in JLS: 'Fans, music and adrenaline!'
Worse thing about being in JLS: 'Not seeing friends and family as much as you'd like to, as we're always busy, always doing something. We go to loads of incredible events and do amazing things and you can't always take your friends and family with you and you want them to see certain things and go to certain places too.'
What Aston would be doing if he wasn't in JLS: 'I would probably be auditioning and if not, already working in entertainment somewhere.'

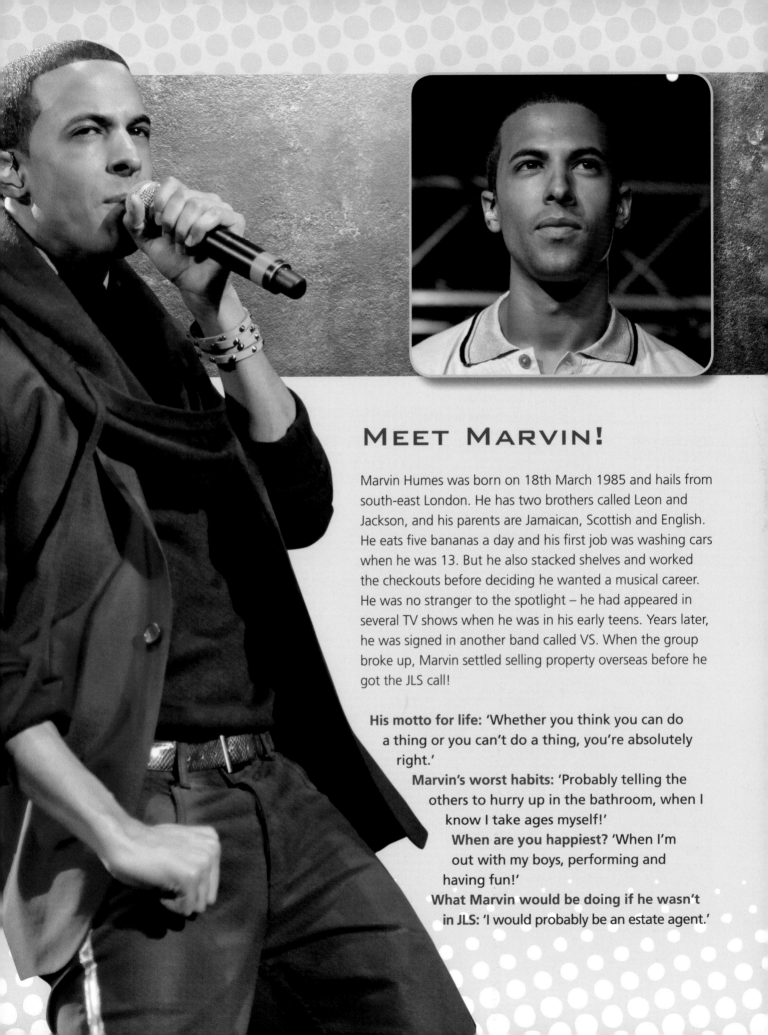

MEET MARVIN!

Marvin Humes was born on 18th March 1985 and hails from south-east London. He has two brothers called Leon and Jackson, and his parents are Jamaican, Scottish and English. He eats five bananas a day and his first job was washing cars when he was 13. But he also stacked shelves and worked the checkouts before deciding he wanted a musical career. He was no stranger to the spotlight – he had appeared in several TV shows when he was in his early teens. Years later, he was signed in another band called VS. When the group broke up, Marvin settled selling property overseas before he got the JLS call!

His motto for life: 'Whether you think you can do a thing or you can't do a thing, you're absolutely right.'

Marvin's worst habits: 'Probably telling the others to hurry up in the bathroom, when I know I take ages myself!'

When are you happiest? 'When I'm out with my boys, performing and having fun!'

What Marvin would be doing if he wasn't in JLS: 'I would probably be an estate agent.'

HEY JB!

Jonathan Benjamin Gill – otherwise known as JB – was born on 7th December 1986, and spent his early years living in Antigua. After that he grew up in Croydon with his brother. Though he didn't have as much professional experience as the other members of the band, JB had been in choirs all the way through school. He played the recorder, piano, flute and guitar at school, but he gave up on music to concentrate on his promising rugby career, playing for London Irish until he was 18. But unfortunately an injury put an end to that, so JB put his energies back into music. His JLS call just sealed his fate! 'It's a tough one to choose, which I would have rather had – Rugby World Cup or No1 with JLS? It would have to be the band I think, but they are very close!' he says.

What makes you angry? 'Dishonesty makes me angry. I don't like it when people aren't real.'
When are you happiest? 'I'm happy when other people are happy. You pick their energy and it lifts your mood.'
What does it mean to be in a band? 'It's all about having fun. When you're in a band you have to enjoy your time together. A lot of people don't get that opportunity – when you're a solo artist you share a journey alone but when you're in a group you share your journey with three or four other people. They're going to go through things that only they'll be able to discuss amongst themselves and they'll share memories that are only ever going to be true to them, that no one else on the outside would be able to really understand.'
What JB would be doing if he wasn't in JLS: 'I would have wanted to play professional rugby but I can't say if I would have ever actually got to that!'

JLS expanding their talents!

'For us, we feel very strongly about doing things that we feel passionate about and also things that we're capable of doing. Two of the boys come from stage school backgrounds and acting is certainly something that we're comfortable doing. We also love to song write and we're capable at doing that and we think we should develop as songwriters as well. It's something that we keep very close to our chests and want to do as often as possible. It's about expanding as people. Obviously, we love our music and that will always be our base, but we love to do other things which are in the creative realm.' **Oritsé**

Yo Oritsé!

Oritsé Williams was born on the 27th November 1986, and his lifelong ambition had always been to be a singer. At primary school the boys used to tease him because he sang in a choir with girls, while the other boys were out playing football. But Oritsé had the last laugh: 'Ladies love a guy who can sing!' he jokes. His favourite albums while he was growing up were *Off The Wall* by Michael Jackson, *Confessions* by Usher and *Songs In The Key Of Life* by Stevie Wonder. Oritsé was a born performer – at aged 15, he used to sing on the school bus. He worked for free at a record company to gain industry experience, and after entering a vocal academy he was persuaded by a mentor to form JLS. And thus, the group was born!

Describing the JLS vibe: 'We're a very well rehearsed band – we're perfectionists – and there's one thing to be talented individuals, but it's another to be a talented group. We always keep on top of each other too, so if any of us aren't on it, the others will just say straight away. It's all to make the best shows possible, and each show has to be better than the previous one.'

Oritsé's motto for life? 'One that is important to me is "Triumph after triumph".'

What Oritsé would be doing if he wasn't in JLS: 'I was in university working with disabled kids so I'd probably still be working with kids and stuff.'

What's on your ipod?

Oritsé: Usher
JB: The Script
Aston: Willow Smith
Marvin: Tinie Tempah

10

WORD SEARCH

```
Q F E Y L T S E C S I P
E B R A L A A I A K A W
A E A D I E S E L I A F
M N L A G R A C T C B A
A J O N A T H E N K L J
A A N R T S S G I S E E
A M D C D N W I M T S S
A I O M U O B N J A S N
E N N D L O G Y R R E M
M A A A A A A A A T D Z
U N I V E R S A L L Y U
H A S M A I L L I W A Q
```

JONATHEN	KICKSTART	LONDON
WILLIAMS	MERRYGOLD	GILL
PISCES	UNIVERSALLY	HUME
DIESEL	BLESSED	BENJAMIN

CHAPTER 2
Musical superstardom

With their slick looks, famous girlfriends and gossip-worthy partying antics, it's almost impossible to imagine the humble beginnings of Oritsé, Marvin, JB and Aston as four regular boys in London with a dream of fame. But that's where they started out. Read on to find out more....

GETTING IT TOGETHER

Though JLS first found fame through *X Factor*, what many people didn't realise was that they were already a band and they hadn't just formed for the purposes of the show. They were four talented guys, determined to get their big break.

The group wasn't your typically manufactured boyband either. While he was studying at university in London in 2007, Oritsé looked at the music scene and had a brain wave that it was the perfect time for a new boyband. He didn't know anyone suitable, but through recommendations from his friends and family, eventually Oritsé met the three lads who would end up forming JLS with him: Aston, Marvin, and JB.

AUDITIONS

Marvin auditioned for Oritsé in the street in Oxford Circus – singing and dancing on the pavement to the whoops and cheers of passers by. Marvin recommended Aston, who he had met at an audition for an advert. The final member to join was JB, whose smooth voice and charismatic style showed him to be the perfect complement to the other three boys.

How did you get your name?

'We were called UFO originally, but we wanted a new name that was a bit sexier. Then we came up with this combination of two things. Do you remember in the 90s there was music in the US called new jack swing? The new jack swing era was a good era, so wouldn't it be great to base our sound on the new jack swing sound? But then we thought that it's too American, and we're not an American band. Then we thought of the British saying 'Jack-the-Lad'. We mixed the two together to create Jack The Lad Swing, which we shortened to JLS, because Jack The Lad Swing was such a mouthful.' **Oritsé**

WORK, WORK, WORK!

The boys started rehearsing together, spending thousands of hours in evenings and weekends in rehearsal studios, working on dance routines, writing songs together, talking about what styles they would wear. They were determined to reach success the old fashioned way – through hard work and talent.

So when friends started suggesting they enter *X Factor*, Oritsé laughed it off as ridiculous. But eventually the boys agreed that any publicity they could get from going on the show would only be a good thing.

All the hours of work they had put in before the show paid off, as the judges were impressed with how slick they were, and also with the brotherly bond that had developed between the boys. JLS sailed through every round to reach the finals of the show, eventually coming in second to bombshell Alexandra Burke.

NEW X FACTOR CONTESTANTS

After their experience of the celebrity show, JLS had some top tips for people who wanted to audition. 'Be confident,' says JB.

'Although it's a completely different process now, in front of a live audience and maybe even backing tracks – it's a lot different to what we've done. I think in a way we've set the barrier for groups. Now they have to learn dance routines for the first audition, all that kind of stuff. Everything that we would bring to the *X Factor*, you have to bring along with you now. I think that's going to bring a big change to the competition. So rehearse – and be confident!'

'These guys, when they came into *X Factor*, they were a great example of how you put a group together, without some old guy saying 'I'm going to put a group together'. It all came from within; they were very rehearsed, very focused, nice people, a great example of how to do it. They're hardworking, they respect their fans and they're super talented.'

SIMON COWELL

CRAZY TIMES – COMING OUT OF THE *X FACTOR* HOUSE

The craziest thing the boys have ever experienced was when they left the *X Factor* house after being on the show. They had been confined in the house for three months and had no idea what was going on outside.

'The first time we came out of the show it was like JLS mayhem. We had our homecoming gig in Croydon, and there were girls tearing down barriers, ripping out each others' hair, trying to climb over things to get to us!' remembers Oritsé. 'We had to have a full police escort, it was seriously unreal. It was like something you'd watch in a movie or something.'

LIFE AFTER *X FACTOR*

As soon as the show was over, JLS were on the road with the *X Factor* live tour, and though there were rumours that Simon Cowell wanted to sign them, nothing ever came of that. Luckily for JLS, Epic Records stepped in and snapped them up. Epic was home to other R&B and urban stars like Lemar and Jay Z, and was the perfect home for the boys.

JLS's catchy debut single 'Beat Again' smashed into the number one spot in the charts, and the boys went off on tour supporting label mate Lemar, where they won themselves thousands more fans in the opening slot. Their hard work was paid off with two MOBO Awards in 2009 for Best Song ('Beat Again') and also Best Newcomer, beating their *X Factor* pal Alexandra Burke.

'We're still a young band with a lot to prove. We had to prove ourselves every week on *X Factor* and then we had to prove we were proper recording artists with our first album. Now we want to prove that wasn't just a fluke, we're here to stay.'

MARVIN

CHART TOPPERS!

Their second single 'Everybody in Love' went to number one too, knocking *X Factor* judge Cheryl Cole off the top spot and their self-entitled debut album *JLS* also topped the UK charts, selling over one million copies. Though the third single from the album, 'One Shot', only reached number six in the UK chart in February 2010, it still sold over 300,000 copies. The group treated their fans to a number of live performances of the song – appearing on Alan Carr's chatshow, *GMTV*, and *Let's Dance* for Sport Relief. And 2010 was to prove to be a lucky year for the boys, as they picked up two Brit Awards – Best Single for 'Beat Again' and Best Breakthrough Act. Pretty special!

'It's fantastic to see how many people are supporting us hoping for us to do well. We've been on tour, so we get screaming fans every day. Although crying always gets to us – we never know whether they're happy or sad!' said JB.

With their eyes firmly set on the future, JLS negotiated a US record deal with Jive Records, and jetted over to the States to start work recording their second album.

On breaking America

'It makes you massively appreciate what you've got back home. We did a gig in a shopping centre in Connecticut about two weeks ago and if we did a shopping centre gig back home it would be crazy. We turned up and there were about ten people there to watch us. It was definitely grounding,' says Marvin.

'Coming to the States this soon wasn't part of our plan. We hoped it might happen in a few years, maybe once we had broken in Europe. Then radio stations started playing our music without knowing who we were. We were offered a deal and asked to come and meet the people supporting us,' said Oritsé.

Marvin added: 'We'll do this for a year or two, or three, if that's what it takes. We'd rather do it right than rush it ... We're having the time of our lives and we're determined to enjoy every second of it.'

MOVING THINGS FORWARD

In early 2010, the boys packed their things and headed off to New York to work with smash hit production team Stargate, who had written some of the biggest club hits in recent years for artists like Beyoncé and Flo Rida. Stargate produced three tracks on the album, including the title track 'Outta This World', 'Love At War' and 'Work'.

The boys were nervous about meeting the production team. 'They're used to working with huge megastars and we're not in that league yet,' said Aston. 'But it was important for us to prove ourselves. We didn't just want to take beats they'd already worked on, we wanted to start from scratch and make something that really represented where we're at.'

JET-SETTING!

The boys then jetted over to LA, to record more material for their second album. The boys were papped stopping for fast food, walking the streets of LA in between rehearsals at the Sony studios and working alongside the same team of songwriters who had written hits like Rihanna's 'Disturbia' and Cheryl Cole's 'Fight For This Love'.

While looking for the inspiration to the songs, each one of the boys looked into their own lives to find things that moved them to write. 'The most important thing when we go into the studio is that we have a theme and a reason for what we're writing,' said Oritsé. 'When we're on the same page we try and put together a joint storyline. We also like to get a vibe from the producers, because often a particular sound of music will inspire a song.'

'Our heroes have got to be our closest family members, because they've taught us manners and respect for other people. Our mums have done great jobs making us well-rounded boys.'

JB

MISSING HOME

But going abroad wasn't all it was cracked up to be. Though the boys were ecstatic to be working on their new album, they also had a serious case of homesickness.

'I miss everyone when I'm away, literally everyone!' said Aston. 'Mum, dad, friends and all our supporters and fans. We miss them too. We miss everyone. This trip I took my DVD collection of *Entourage* with me – Marvin and I really got into it and watched all six series in about six weeks! It had to be done.'

As well as working on their second album, JLS also put their dancing feet to work, playing gigs and doing interviews across the country to try and replicate their UK success, visiting Chicago, Rhode Island, Milwaukee, Philadelphia and New York. Busy boys! They returned to LA later in the year to record a video for the single 'Love You More', and were greeted at the airport by scores of American paparazzi.

'The best advice anyone ever gave me was work hard, and keep going with your dream. You'll be told no 10 times before you get a yes and you get a chance.'
MARVIN

Who are JLS tipping for superstardom? Jessie J!

'Our country's never had anything like Jessie, she's got that kind of pop iconic appeal, in the same way that Madonna had and Lady Gaga has for the rest of the world. I think that for someone like Jessie she's just the realist artist that you can find. She's a really nice, good-hearted person.' **Oritsé**

CELEBRITY LIFESTYLE

It didn't take them long to slot in with the Hollywood way of life, going out for dinner with N'Sync and rubbing shoulders with countless other celebrities.

'We were hanging out with Katy Perry, Adam Lambert and Justin Bieber – it's just crazy the amount of people you bump into!' said Aston. 'It was funny when we were with Justin Bieber actually, he said hello to us all and then Marvin said: "Allo mate, how you doin'? You alright?" and Justin turned around and said back to him in a cockney accent: "Allo mate, how you doin'? You alright?" It was the funniest thing, seeing this young Canadian guy putting on a cockney accent. It was hilarious!'

Their tour of America took in some of the country's theme parks, which was an amazing experience for the boys, who would turn up, do the soundcheck, go on stage, and then have the freedom of the park, which was left open for the boys an hour after they played! The boys made sure they went on the log flume (Oritsé's favourite ride) and posted a photo of them in the Texas Six Flags on their Twitter page.

DESIGN YOUR OWN JLS FAN T-SHIRT

Are you the biggest JLS superfan? Express your creative talents by designing your own JLS T-shirt using our patterns below!

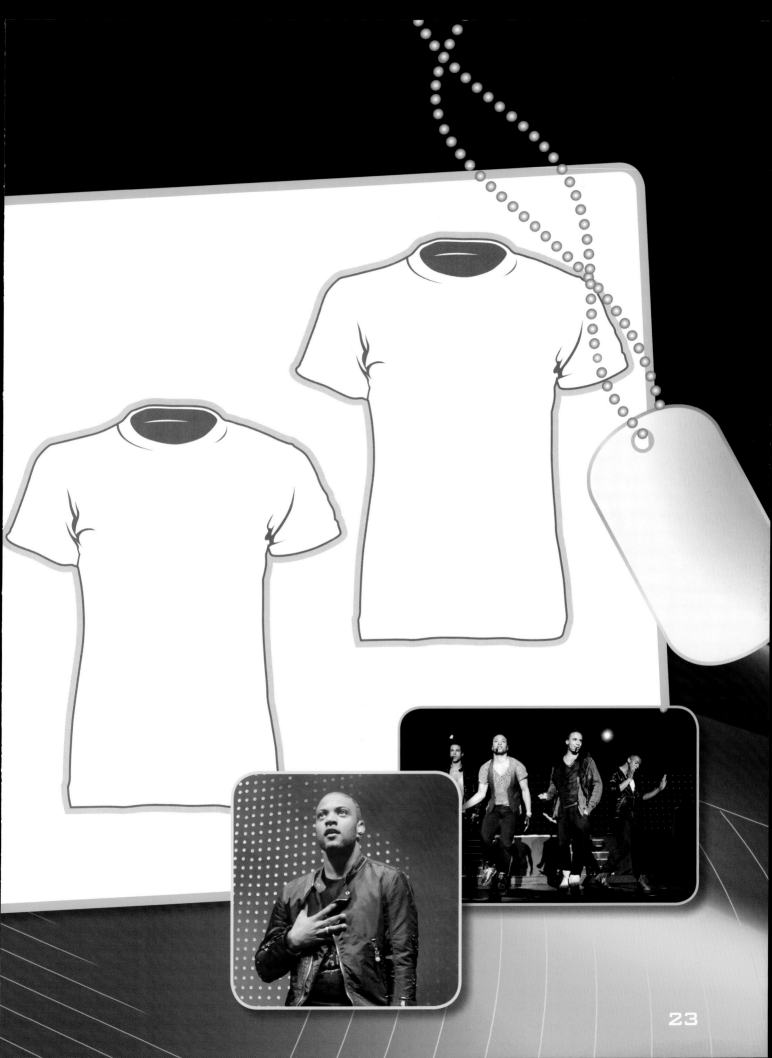

THE SINGLES

'THE CLUB IS ALIVE'

JLS introduced their second album with the single 'The Club Is Alive', released in July 2010. The song took its lead lyric from the Julie Andrews musical 'The Sound of Music', but the two things couldn't have been musically more apart! The track was written by Savan Kotecha, who had previously worked with Britney Spears, Leona Lewis and Alexandra Burke. When Savan presented the idea to the boys, they were initially sceptical. But after having worked on it in the studio for a couple of days, the boys were sold. 'The Club Is Alive' combined a smooth beat with ravey productions, and it got good reviews across the board. It smashed into the UK charts at number one, giving JLS their third number one hit and going on to sell a quarter of a million copies. Incredible!

'To be honest we try not to think about the fame because then you get above your station. It's best to try not to get sucked into the hype too much. It's about the music and everything else is a bonus'.
ASTON

'LOVE YOU MORE'

Having announced that they were well and truly back, the second single to be released from the album was a slower tempo love song called 'Love You More'. The song was written by JLS with producers Wayne Hector and Toby Gad. It was never supposed to be a single, but after JLS were approached to release the official Children in Need 2010 single, they agreed that 'Love You More' was the most suitable track on the album for the event. The song shot into the UK chart at number one, giving JLS their fourth number one single! And ever the generous bunch, the boys donated 100% of the profits and proceeds to Children in Need.

'EYES WIDE SHUT'

The final single to be released from the album was 'Eyes Wide Shut', featuring fellow London talent, rapper Tinie Tempah.

'Tinie killed it on the track!' said Marvin. 'It was a track that we'd written first of all in LA, last summer. We'd tried to work with Tinie for a long time. We were either going to feature on something of his or vice versa you know, he heard the track and he wanted to jump on it. Then we got to shoot a video with him. People don't think he was actually at the video shoot but he was. It was an amazing video for us, and you know everyone

'We're very proud to be doing British pop-R&B. I think it is different from the American style. Usher is an incredible act and we all respect him very highly. If it wasn't for someone like Taio Cruz, then we wouldn't be where we are right now, having the opportunities that are in front of us. For us, our music is different from American music and I think there's room for all types of music.'
ORITSÉ

Favourite tracks on *Outta This World*

Marvin: 'I Know What She Like'
Oritsé: 'Outta This World'
JB: 'Private War'
Aston: 'Superhero'

THE ALBUM

OUTTA THIS WORLD

The release of 'Love You More' coincided with the long-awaited release of the band's second album, *Outta This World*. They had spent months in the studio, working alongside some of the greatest contemporary musical talent – producers, audio engineers, songwriters – and now, the final product was completed and unleashed on the public.

'The album is diverse,' explained JB. 'With our new single, again people are saying that it's something we've never done before, but songs like *Crazy For You* and *Tightrope* from our last album were also stripped back. It's reflective of our feelings and our thought process. It's got a bit of a different flavour but it still has the JLS stamp.'

The album went into the UK album chart at number two and into the Irish chart at number four, and sold over 150,000 copies in its first week alone. Wow! Reviews of the album were varied, but overall, it proclaimed the arrival of a serious force in the boyband scene. Having shrugged off the X Factor baggage they were previously attached to, *Now* magazine heralded '*Outta This World* is a bold affirmation of JLS's arrival as a pop force.' And not a moment too soon!

TAKING A RISK

For the boys, the album was a bold step in a new direction. 'The most important thing that we did on the second album is that musically we took risks,' says Oritsé. 'A lot of people might have thought we'd just repeat what we've done before, but we've grown from the first album to the second album … we took house tracks and wrote to them, we took R&B tracks, pop tracks, acoustic tracks.

We just went in on any type of music genre we could find and if something came out of that we thought was special, we went back and recorded it. I definitely think it's going to bring in more fans that maybe weren't listening to our music before.'

The boys rewarded their fans – who had waited patiently for the release of the second album – with a series of in-store signings around the country. Time after time, Aston, Marvin, JB and Oritsé were greeted by hundreds of screaming JLS female fans who had queued in the streets waiting to see their heroes.

The album was released with different covers – one for each of the boys. 'We all had a bet on who would sell the most. I know it's going to be me!' joked Aston.

Hitting Back

Though the boys don't take award nominations too seriously, they were a little miffed to be nominated for Worst Band at the 2011 NME Awards. 'I'm actually happy that we made it in,' said Oritsé. 'Whether it's for a good thing or a bad thing, we've been recognised. But to be totally honest, I was disappointed that NME would even put us up for that award because we've brought something really significant to music. We also do a lot of charity work. So if NME think JLS are the worst band for all the good we're trying to do, I'd have to question them.'

LIFE ON TOUR

Within days of the release of the album *Outta This World*, the boys set off on a series of arena tours around the UK, playing a gruelling schedule of 39 shows across England, Ireland, Scotland and Wales between November 2010 and January 2011.

The *Outta This World* show opened with the boys in a flying car singing the title track from the album *Outta This World*. They then jumped out of the car and onto the bonnet where they performed a dance routine, to the screams and applause of the crowd. Out of the flying car, the boys then launched into their best-loved tunes, including 'Everybody In Love' and 'Beat Again',

'We don't really have any diva habits but all we ask for is an hour to ourselves before we go on stage because we need to be in the right mindset. When you're rushing around all day and you have people to meet and promotions and stuff, we just want an hour to chill out and do vocal warm up.'

JB

'The one city that goes absolutely bonkers for us, outside of London, is Glasgow. We've been there many times now: on the *X Factor* tour, on tour with Lemar and doing our own private gigs up there and they're just crazy. The people in Glasgow are just brilliant.'
JB

Off stage and back at the tour bus, the boys had been keeping up their reputation for being cheeky, by playing a number of pranks on each other. The first rule on the bus was that no-one was allowed to sleep during the day 'No one's allowed to go to sleep during what we call working hours, which is on the bus during the day to and from venues,' said Aston. 'Whoever does, something unpleasant will happen. A dancer fell asleep so we took pictures, it wasn't pretty. The only think we have promised not to do is shave eyebrows off!'

RECORDING THE THIRD ALBUM!

No sooner had *Outta This World* hit the charts than the JLS boys were back in the studio, discussing the making of their third album. 'We're going to be working with Bruno Mars,' revealed Marvin. 'Bruno's had the biggest song of the year so far and he's not only a great writer but a great artist too. Hopefully we'll duet with him but we will also be writing with him at some point this year too.'

All this on top of a string of tour dates and a 3D movie! Where on earth do they find the time??

What is your favourite song to sing on tour?

JB: '"Eyes Wide Shut" is my favourite song to sing live. I absolutely love the lyrics, production, dance routine and vibe from start to finish!'

Marvin: '"Love You More" … just because we're on the walkway and that song is dedicated to each and every single person in those arenas. It's such an emotional moment for me in the show!'

Oritsé: '"Eyes Wide Shut". The reaction from the audience was always incredible and the routine is always amazing to perform. Also Tinie Tempah makes a special appearance and it gives a moment in the show like no other song, especially as it is our only collaboration of the night.'

Aston: 'My favourite song to sing is "That's My Girl", or the cover we do, "Somebody To Love".'

'Without sounding clichéd, our fans mean the world to us. They are absolutely everything to us. We believe we've got the best supporters in the country. In terms of their dedication and their support for us, it's second to none. Our fans are crazy, but good crazy!'
ASTON

J♥S

LOVELOVELOVELOVELOVELOVELOVELOVELOVE
LOVELOVELOVELOVELOVELOVELOVELOVELOVE
LOVELOVELOVELOVELOVELOVELOVELOVELOVE
LOVELOVELOVELOVELOVELOVELOVELOVELOVE

YOUR JLS SCRAPBOOK

An awesome way to keep everything together about your favourite member of JLS is to start your own JLS scrapbook! It's a super easy way of keeping all the great bits of gossip together, as well as gorgeous pictures …

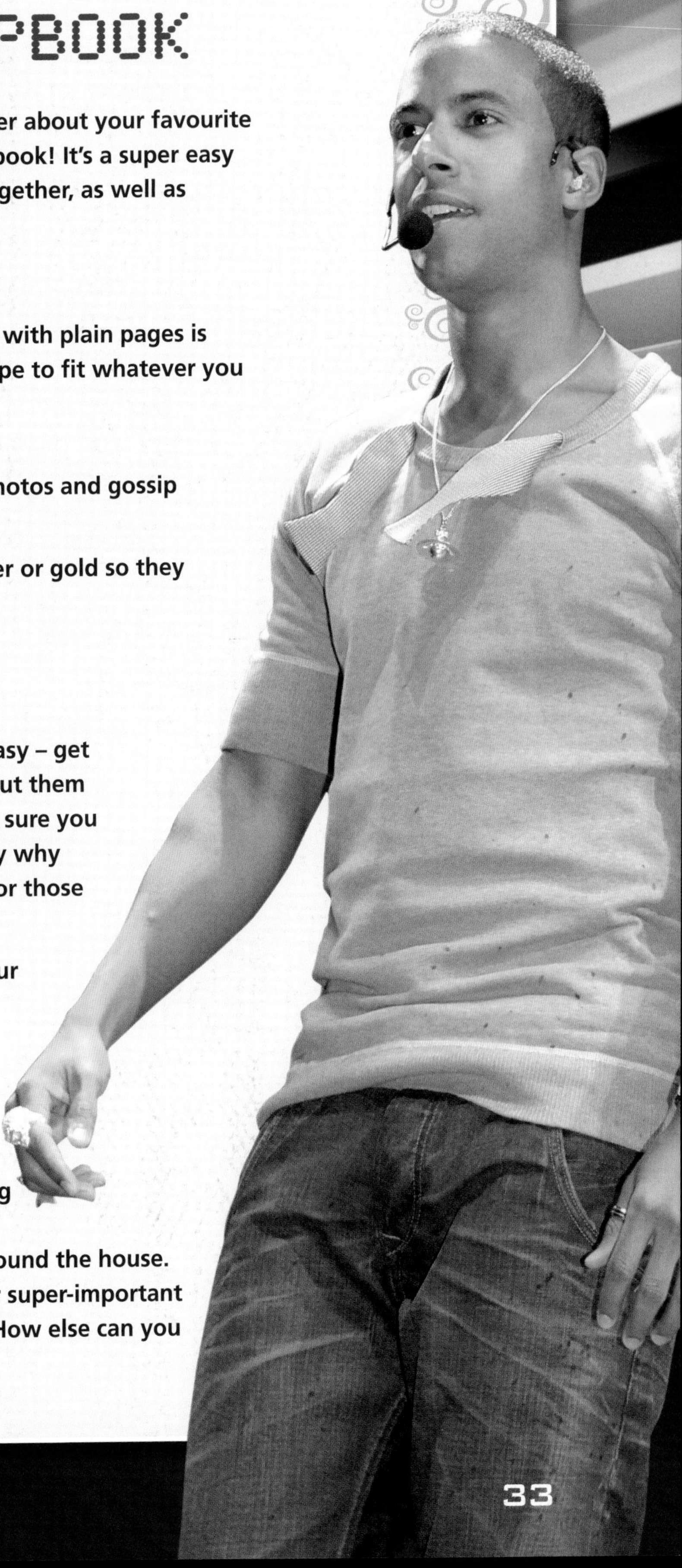

You will need:

✔ A book to use as a scrapbook. Something with plain pages is best, but you can choose the size and shape to fit whatever you personally like

✔ Sticky tape, glue and scissors

✔ Celeb magazines featuring loads of JLS photos and gossip

✔ Photos of JLS printed from the internet

✔ Some nice marker pens (perhaps red, silver or gold so they really stand out)

✔ Optional extras: glitter, ribbons

What to do:

The theory of scrapbooking is really pretty easy – get together a load of images and information, cut them out, and stick them in your scrapbook! Make sure you write on each page, so you remember exactly why you included those photos of Aston's pecs – or those photos of JB's cheeky smile!

There are tons of ways you can embellish your scrapbook pages using glitter and ribbons. Experiment with pasting glue over images and then shaking glitter over the glue so it gets stuck down and adds a twinkle to your scrapbook pages.

You can buy all sorts of exciting scrapbooking supplies, but really, you can make a great scrapbook with stationary you have lying around the house. It's the perfect way to keep together all your super-important information about Oritsé's favourite foods! How else can you truly be a JLS superfan?

TAKE THE JLS QUIZ!

1. Which Michael Jackson song did JLS sing on the *X Factor*?

a 'Thriller'
b 'You Are Not Alone'
c 'ABC'
d 'The Way you make me Feel'

2. What is Aston's middle name?

a Fred
b Luke
c Allen
d Ian

3. What was their second number one single called?

a 'Everybody in Love'
b 'Love Ain't Here Anymore'
c 'Love Again'
d 'Put your Hands Up'

4. Where has Aston got a tattoo and what is it of?

a Back – A musical note
b Arm – Celtic band
c Wrist – JLS
d Bum – Devil

5. What is Marvin's star sign?

a Capricorn
b Gemini
c Taurus
d Pisces

6. When is Aston's birthday?

a 29th December 1988
b 13th February 1988
c 1st March 1988
d 30th March 1988

7. Which children's TV show did Aston star in?

a *Big Cook Little Cook*
b *Something Special*
c *Jackanory Junior*
d *The Fun Song Factory*

8. Which Christmas song did JLS sing in the *X Factor* final?

a 'Merry Christmas Everyone'
b 'Last Christmas'
c 'Walking in the Air'
d 'Do they know it's Christmas?'

9. Who did Aston appear as in *Stars in their Eyes*?

a Ray Charles
b Michael Jackson
c Lionel Richie
d Stevie Wonder

34

10. What is their autobiography called?

a JLS

b JLS – Our Story So Far

c JLS – Beat Again

d JLS – The Beginning

11. What does Oritsé mean?

a Lucky one

b Gifted

c Universally blessed

d Charmed

12. Who is scared of dogs?

a Aston

b Oritsé

c Marvin

d JB

13. What order were JLS founded?

a Oritsé, Marvin, Aston and JB

b Marvin, JB, Oritsé, Aston

c JB, Marvin, Oritsé, Aston

d Aston, Marvin, JB, Oritsé

14. Which member played the trumpet as a child?

a Aston

b Oritsé

c Marvin

d JB

15. Whose last name is Gill?

a Aston

b Oritsé

c Marvin

d JB

16. Why did the creator of JLS (Oritsé) start the band?

a Fame

b For a bet

c Pay for mum's healthcare

d Just for fun

17. Which city were the boys born in?

a Newcastle

b Leeds

c London

d Birmingham

18. What is JLS's fave restaurant?

a Wagamama

b Nandos

c Giraffe

d Pizza Express

19. What was the first concert Marvin went to?

a Bon Jovi

b Brian Adams

c Tina Turner

d Michael Jackson

20. What year did JLS come second in the X Factor?

a 2007

b 2004

c 2008

d 2006

CHAPTER 3
Love Stuff

Of course, when you're a trendy boyband that just oozes talent, there's always going to be no end of beautiful women throwing themselves at you. There have been so many rumours of romantic engagements – but find out what's really going on in the love lives of our four favourite boys!

ASTON

Though Aston arguably gets the most female attention, he's not had the greatest luck with ladies. He wants to experience true love like bandmate Marvin. 'It's true love, isn't it?' said Aston about Marvin and Rochelle. 'It's lovely, like a fairytale. It makes you a little bit sick because you haven't got it, though!'

Although he's surrounded by screaming fans all the time, Aston thinks that since the group appeared on *X Factor*, it's much more difficult to meet the right girl. 'It's a lot harder since the *X Factor* as you can't trust anyone. I only trust the guys I work with and my mum,' he says.

'Maybe my perfect lady will come along soon,' says Aston. 'There's hope for that.' And hope for all of us too!

Q. What looks do you love on a girl?

'I love open toe shoes, and I hate kitten heels. Go flat, or go high. No inbetween!' **Marvin**

'I love wedges on girls!' **JB**

'Baggy leggings. If you're going to wear leggings, wear them so they fit. That's how they're supposed to be worn.' **Aston**

'My taste changes every so often but I have to be with a girl who can keep up with my life'
ASTON

JB

Though he's not seen in the gossip columns as much as the other boys, JB has been with his girlfriend Chloe since they met when JLS competed in *X Factor*. Chloe is a dancer, who danced with JLS during the competition.

'I've been with my girlfriend for a while now,' says JB. 'She lives in Epsom, about 15 minutes away from me and I see her all the time. I like the way she thinks. To me, that's more important than what you wear or how much money you earn. I think she's got her priorities right.'

'They have gone to great lengths to keep things quiet,' said a friend of the couple. 'They always arrive and leave separately when they're out. But they've been an item since she danced with JLS on the *X Factor* in 2008. They're very good together. She completely understands the business JB is in.

'If I got married I wouldn't want an OK! style wedding, but it would be huge though. I'd have to invite everybody'.

JB

The JLS valentine's mix tape:

If you're looking for a selection of smooth tunes to woo that special someone, check this out – the official JLS word on love songs!

Maxwell: 'This Woman's Work'

Brian McKnight: 'I Do'

Alicia Keys: 'Butterflies'

Sara Bareilles: 'Gravity'

Boyz II Men: 'Water Runs Dry'

Mario: 'Let Me Love You'

Beyoncé: 'Smash Into You'

MARVIN

Marvin started dating Rochelle Wiseman of The Saturdays after they met at an Alicia Keys album launch in 2009. They went public with their relationship a few months later, and were papped together – on dates, holidays, and nights out partying on the town.

'They're such a great couple,' gushed Rachel's bandmate Frankie. 'I don't believe in being with someone if you don't believe they couldn't be that special person,' said Marvin. The two were inseparable, and even though they had only been together a few months, they were already talking about moving in together. 'I'm very loved-up. She's an incredible girl. She's extremely thoughtful and very generous to everyone,' said Marvin.

Time out

But the fairytale wasn't to last. After a few months of bliss, soon cracks started appearing in the couple's relationship, which were caused by the hectic schedules of JLS and The Saturdays. Marvin took to the JLS Twitter to confirm the rumours: 'I'm very sad to say that it is all true. Rochelle and I have split up. Thank you for all your kind messages of support. Love you guys. Marv x.'

But after less than two months apart, they were spotted together in early 2011 when Marvin picked Rochelle up from The Saturdays tour rehearsal. The couple tried to hide their faces, but they were papped in Marvin's car. The love birds have been careful not to spill too much about the relationship, but we hope they have worked it out!

'It sounds cliché, but I never like a girl until I get to know them. Just because someone is good looking it doesn't mean they're nice. I've only really fancied people I've got to know.'
MARVIN

ORITSÉ

Like the other JLS boys, Oritsé is an old romantic at heart – but he's been focusing all his attentions on the band for so long that he hasn't had time to factor in a girlfriend.

When it comes to his taste in women, Oritsé loves the high-waisted jeans look on a girl. He also loves baggy trousers and cargo pants. But he's not one for extravagant make-up – he likes girls to keep it minimal, with a lash of lip gloss. He's terrified of huge extravagant fake eyelashes too, so make sure you aren't wearing any when you're on your first date with him!

Oritsé has had his fair share of bad experiences. The worst date he ever went on was with a girl who said absolutely nothing to him, but then launched herself on him! 'My lips were so red afterwards. Terrible!'

The search is on!

Having his close buddies Marvin and JB both being head over heels in love has left Oritsé feeling like he wants some love too. 'I'm super-ambitious, so I've been caught up in JLS for ages. I'm having the greatest time. But maybe it's time I got a bit of romance. I want a down-to-earth, fun-loving girl.'

Once, when Oritsé was younger, he saved as much cash as he could then splashed out, spending all of it on a limousine ride to impress a girl. He was determined to arrange a special treat for the lady in his life, but unfortunately he couldn't save quite enough for the limo, and had to persuade the driver to give him a discount!

'I had no money at the time but still wanted to do something very special for this girl who I thought I was in love with at the time ... So I went to this limousine place and told the guy I only had £200, which I had been saving for months. He just looked at me and said I was crazy, but I eventually convinced him and managed to take my girl for a limo tour of London for the night!' What a sweetheart!

'It's not easy to meet girls who you would actually want to be with. It's hard to trust people as you don't know what their intentions are'
ORITSÉ

Q. Have you ever been sent a weird Valentine's present by a fan?

'Yes, themselves! A girl posted herself to my house and gave me a rose.' **Oritsé**

WHICH MEMBER OF JLS ARE YOU MOST LIKELY TO DATE?

Answer all the questions below, then check our handy score chart to see which member of JLS you're best suited to!

What qualities *do* you look for in a man?

- ◯ Friendly, honest and loyal, original and independent
- ◯ Imaginative, sensitive, kind, sympathetic and selfless
- ◯ Optimistic, happy, freedom-loving, honest
- ◯ Intellectual, deep, introspective

What's your favourite film?

- ◯ *The Matrix*
- ◯ *Coming to America*
- ◯ *The Lion King*
- ◯ *Rush Hour*

Where *do* you like your man to shop for clothes?

- ◯ Burberry
- ◯ Topman
- ◯ Selfridges, London
- ◯ New Era

What's your ideal holiday destination?

- ◯ Florida
- ◯ Caribbean
- ◯ Antigua
- ◯ Thailand

What's your favourite animal?

- ◯ Koala
- ◯ Lion
- ◯ Eagle
- ◯ Monkey

Describe your perfect man's style:

- ◯ Sometimes cool, chilling, sophisticated, slick, sweetboy!
- ◯ 'Jents Looking Sick!' (JLS)
- ◯ Sexy, cool, retro, different, unique
- ◯ Urban gentleman

And now, how about your style?

○ You're a real smart cookie – more about substance than style. You'd rather hit the books than the clubs. But you're still smoking hot, and you know it!

○ You're a glamour puss at heart. You love nothing more than dressing up to the nines, making sure you look the part. You're always seen in towering heels and micro skirts. But you've got a big heart too.

○ You're the cheeky one in your group – you like playing tricks on your friends, staying out late and partying. But you've always got the back of your friends and family.

○ You're a hot shot. You're totally focused on your career but you love to have fun – you just need to be reminded of that sometimes …

What's your favourite colour?

○ **Red**

○ **Green**

○ **Blue**

○ **Yellow**

Who should you date?

Tot up the number of answers you scored in each colour, then check out the chart below

If you had more Red then your man is Oritsé

if you picked Green then you are destined to date Marvin

if you picked Blue then you and Aston will be in love forever

and if you picked Yellow, then it's you and JB!

THROW A JLS PARTY!

What better theme for a sleepover than throwing a JLS party?? You and your friends will have the most awesome evening ever.

Just follow our instructions to maximise your JLS fun!

You will need:

✔ your friends

✔ posters and pictures of JLS

✔ MP3 player and speakers/stereo, plus the two JLS albums, *JLS* and *Outta This World*

✔ munchie food (we recommend fried chicken in honour of the boys' Nando obsession, plus cupcakes, fruit, and the recipes for the JLS shakes found in this book)

✔ drawing paper and pens

✔ pyjamas

What to do:

To throw yourself a dandy little JLS party, you need to set the scene. Make sure your bedroom walls are plastered with posters of JLS (though they probably already are, lol!), set up your speakers and start blasting the first album.

Of course, you'll all have to do the dance moves for 'Beat Again', so when that comes on the stereo, drop what you're doing and do the heartbeat move!

Get yourself in the kitchen and check out our recipes for JLS shakes – pick your favourite member of JLS and make yourself their favourite flavour shake!

Use the paper and pens to design JLS T-shirts. You can then copy your favourite design into the JLS T-Shirt design activity in this book!

Once you've listened to JLS all the way through, then listen to *Outta This World*. Careful not to blow your speakers or annoy your parents and siblings with the loud music!

CHAPTER 4
JLS – Smokin' style!

Though it's a long time since the boys first started out in the business, they've always made sure to co-ordinate their outfits and make sure they keep that special JLS flavour when they're performing. And things haven't changed that much now – except they have an army of stylists and wardrobe assistants to make the job slightly easier!

Mirror, mirror!

And even though all the boys like to take care of themselves in terms of looks, there's one member who spends a lot longer than the others in front of the mirror: Oritsé! 'I like to take care of myself and I like what I wear to reflect my character, so yeah, I take the longest, fair enough! It's not a bad thing,' he says.

When the boys are getting ready, it's Aston who's always ready first, even though he has to spend time straightening his hair. He's not ashamed of owning straightening irons either. 'They're good enough for David Beckham, they're good enough for me!' he jokes.

Even though they're all naturally sporty, the boys make sure to stay in shape when they're on the road and at home by working out. 'We find it easy to keep in shape when we're on tour. We're on stage for nearly two hours so we've got that advantage. We're lucky,' says Marvin.

What's their scent?

JB - Gucci Pour Homme
Marvin - Calvin Klein - Eternity
Aston - Paco Rabanne Smile
Oritsé - Issey Miyake

49

THAT PLUNGING NECKLINE ...

The boys like to make a statement when they're out, and usually you'll see them in matching outfits, even when they're off stage. They all sport smooth waxed chests which you can see quite clearly when they wear their signature low v-neck t-shirts, exposing some serious man cleavage – or he-vage!

The low v-neck was quite a hit with singers in the 1970s, but JLS are bringing the look back, along with other stars like Russell Brand, Jude Law and Gossip Girl star Ed Westwick. Even Marvin's missus Rochelle Wiseman sometimes thinks the trend has gone too far! 'I turn round and say, "Er, isn't that a bit low?" But that's his thing. The ladies love it. He loves a low-cut top. He's got a good chest. So we'll let him get it out. He doesn't wax but his chest is as smooth as a baby's bum.'

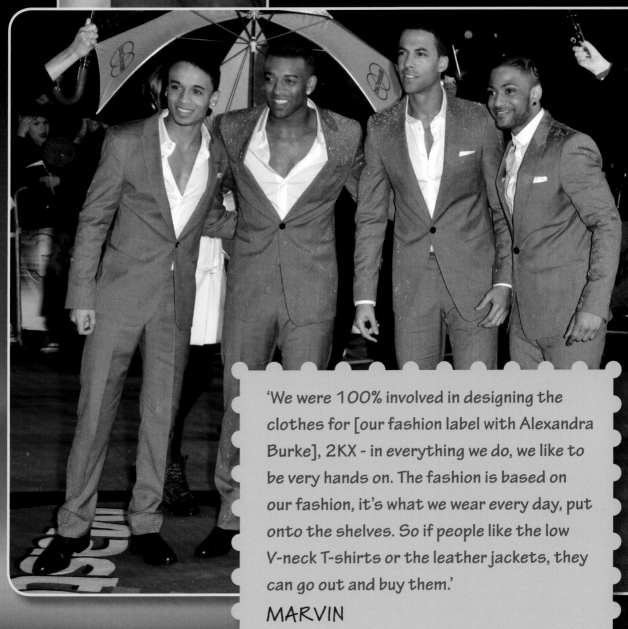

'We were 100% involved in designing the clothes for [our fashion label with Alexandra Burke], 2KX - in everything we do, we like to be very hands on. The fashion is based on our fashion, it's what we wear every day, put onto the shelves. So if people like the low V-neck T-shirts or the leather jackets, they can go out and buy them.'

MARVIN

What's their secret?

In only the first year of their recording careers, JLS had three UK number one singles, over 4 times platinum debut album, two 2009 MOBO Awards and two 2010 BRIT awards. So, what's the secret to their success?

'If I had to put my finger on it, I think people can see the genuine bond we have between us,' says Marvin. We genuinely are best friends and genuinely love what we do and that's something you can't manufacture.

It's real.'

What does the future hold? 'There's always something new to achieve, there's always records to be broken, always new things to do. If you think, "I've done everything, sit back", then you are done. You can always learn something, have a goal to strive towards.'
ASTON

53

CROSSWORD

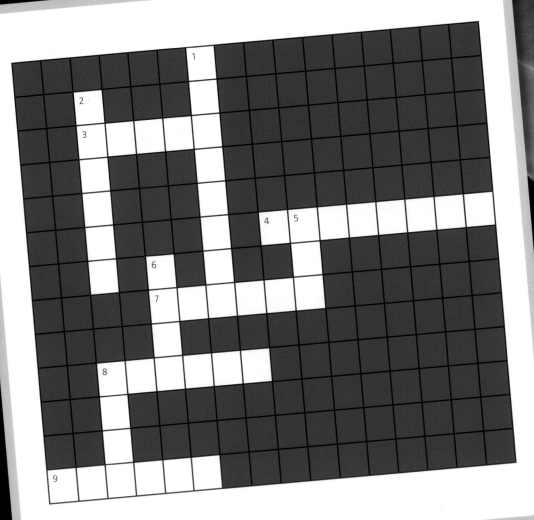

Across

3. Who played the trumpet as a child?
4. What is Ortisé's last name?
7. Where are the boys from?
8. What was Aston's nickname before JLS?
9. What is Marvin's star sign?

Down

1. What does the J stand for in JB?
2. What is the bands' fave restaurant?
5. What is Aston's middle name?
6. What is Aston's Favourite colour ?
8. What is Aston scared of?

CODE CRACKER!

Decipher the code and discover your secret JLS messages! Each letter has been replaced by a symbol, so use the guide and find out how your really feel. You can even use the symbols to write your own secret messages to the boys!

A	B	C	D	E	F	G	H	I	J	K	L	M
✡	✛	✤	✣	✥	◆	◇	★	☆	☉	✩	✬	✫

N	O	P	Q	R	S	T	U	V	W	X	Y	Z
✭	✮	☆	✳	✴	✶	✷	✸	✹	✺	✻	✼	✵

MAKE YOUR JLS SHAKE!

The JLS boys love tucking into healthy shakes after they've finished a workout. Check out these four tasty recipes, each one for a different member of the group!

ASTON'S SPICED BANANA SHAKE

This tasty banana shake is the perfect thing for cooling down on hot days!

You need:

- ✔ 1 ripe banana
- ✔ 1 cup cold milk (use soy milk if you are allergic to dairy)
- ✔ 3 tablespoons vanilla ice cream or vanilla yoghurt (optional)
- ✔ ground cinnamon or nutmeg

What to do:

Put the banana, milk and ice cream or yoghurt into a bowl and whisk with an electric mixer. Blend until the mixture is smooth and creamy. Pour into a tall glass and sprinkle with cinnamon or nutmeg.

MARVIN'S CREAMY CHOCOLATE SHAKE

This creamy chocolate shake is a real indulgence – just like our Marv!

You need:

- ✔ 2 scoops chocolate ice cream
- ✔ 1 cup cold milk
- ✔ 2 tablespoons of crushed chocolate (you can use normal milk chocolate and crush it using the back of a spoon)
- ✔ a strawberry (optional, for garnish)

What to do:

Put the ice cream, milk and chocolate into a bowl and whisk with an electric mixer. Blend until the mixture is smooth and creamy. Pour into a tall glass and sprinkle with a little crushed chocolate and a strawberry.

ORITSÉ'S PEACHY DELIGHT SHAKE

Oritsé's shake of choice is this peachy delight shake. And once you taste it, you'll see why!

You need:

- ✔ 200g sliced tinned peaches
- ✔ quarter cup pineapple juice
- ✔ 2 scoops vanilla ice cream
- ✔ half a cup of milk

What to do:

Put the peaches and pineapple juice in the blender and mix until smooth. Add the ice cream and blend again until the mixture is soft, then add the milk and mix until it's all mixed together.

JB'S STRAWBERRY SURPRISE SHAKE

Strawberry Surprise is JB's favourite shake flavour. Make your own following this simple recipe.

You need:

- ✔ 250g fresh strawberries
- ✔ 1 cup cold milk
- ✔ 1 ripe banana

What to do:

Wash the strawberries and make sure you remove the stalks. Put the strawberries and the banana into a blender and mix until smooth and creamy.

LOOKING FORWARD

When you think of what JLS have achieved in such a short space of time, it's quite incredible. Number one smash hit singles, two best selling albums, sell out arena tours playing to thousands and thousands of screaming fans.

But there's still so much the boys want to do. They've got a huge wish list of people they want to collaborate with on future material: Rihanna, Jay-Z, Usher, Drake, The Script, Beyoncé. And although they've begun their quest to conquer America, there's still a long way to go before they reach the same level of popularity they have achieved in the UK.

But these boys are in no rush because they know that slow and steady wins the race. 'We just take every day as it comes,' says JB. 'That was what we did on *X Factor* – just prepared for what we had to do in the here and now. But of course, we've got our sights on the horizon too. We know what we want to achieve. We just have to get there.'

And the boys have countless new secret projects that they're working on. Another clothing range, a 3D movie, and of course, their third album! The boys have hooked up with some of the same producers who worked on album number two, with sensational results!

One thing is for certain, JLS definitely aren't splitting up to go solo. The boys made a commitment to music, and none of them have plans to steal the limelight – not yet, anyway.

'If JLS ever does end – which it won't – it'll be all four of us deciding to end it,' says Marvin. 'We'll be friends forever. The group works and we're happy as we are.'
And long may it continue!

ANSWERS

Wordsearch – page 11

Q	F	E	Y	L	T	S	E	C	S	I	P
E	B	R	A	L	A	A	I	A	K	A	W
A	E	A	D	I	E	S	E	L	I	A	F
M	N	L	A	G	R	A	C	T	C	B	A
A	J	O	N	A	T	H	E	N	K	L	J
A	A	N	R	T	S	S	G	I	S	E	E
A	M	D	C	D	N	W	I	M	T	S	S
A	I	O	M	U	O	B	N	J	A	S	N
E	N	N	D	L	O	G	Y	R	R	E	M
M	A	A	A	A	A	A	A	A	T	D	Z
U	N	I	V	E	R	S	A	L	L	Y	U
H	A	S	M	A	I	L	L	I	W	A	Q

JLS Crossword – page 54

Across

3. Aston
4. Williams
7. London
8. Diesel
9. Pisces

Down

1. Jonathen
2. Nandos
5. Ian
6. Blue
8. Dogs

Quiz – page 35

1. d 'The Way You Make Me Feel'
2. d Ian
3. a 'Everybody in Love'
4. a Back- A musical note
5. d Pisces
6. b 13th February 1988
7. d *The Fun Song Factory*
8. b 'Last Christmas'
9. b Michael Jackson
10. b *JLS – Our Story So Far*
11. c Universally blessed
12. a Aston
13. a Oritsé, Marvin, Aston and JB
14. a Aston
15. d JB
16. c Pay for mum's healthcare
17. c London
18. b Nandos
19. d Michael Jackson
20. a 2007

Code Cracker – page 55

JLS ARE MY FAVOURITE
YOU MAKE MY HEART BEAT AGAIN
I LOVE ASTON THE MOST
JLS ARE THE BEST BAND
JLS ARE AMAZING
I WANT TO MARRY ASTON
NO ONE IS LIKE JLS
I AM THE ULTIMATE JLS FAN
I LOVE ALL OF JLS
I WISH I COULD DANCE LIKE JLS

PICTURE CREDITS

All pictures courtesy of Getty Images

ACKNOWLEDGEMENTS

Posy Edwards would like to thank Helia Phoenix, Jane Sturrock, Nicola Crossley, Helen Ewing, Rich Carr and Briony Hartley.

First published in hardback in Great Britain in 2010 by Orion Books an imprint of the Orion Publishing Group Ltd Orion House, 5 Upper St Martin's Lane, London WC2H 9EA An Hachette UK Company

10 9 8 7 6 5 4 3 2 1

A CIP catalogue record for this book is available from the British Library.

ISBN: 978 4091 4125 9

Designed by Goldust Design
Printed in Italy by Rotolito Lombarda

The Orion Publishing Group's policy is to use papers that are natural, renewable and recyclable and made from wood grown in sustainable forests. The logging and manufacturing processes are expected to conform to the environmental regulations of the country of origin.

Every effort has been made to fulfil requirements with regard to reproducing copyright material. The author and publisher will be glad to rectify any omissions at the earliest opportunity.

www.orionbooks.co.uk